Assi Manifesto

poems

Natasha Kanapé Fontaine

translated by

Howard Scott

D1299972

MAWENZI
HOUSE

We acknowledge the support of the Canada Council for the Arts for our publishing program. We also acknowledge support from the Government of Ontario through the Ontario Arts Council.

We acknowledge the financial support of the Government of Canada through the National Translation Program for Book Publishing, an initiative of the *Roadmap for Canada's Official Languages 2013-2018: Education, Immigration, Communities*, for our translation activities.

Previously published in a French edition as *Manifeste Assi* by Mémoire d'encrier, Montreal, Quebec.

Cover design by Sabrina Pignataro

Library and Archives Canada Cataloguing in Publication
Kanapé Fontaine, Natasha, 1991-
[Manifeste Assi. English]
    Assi manifesto / Natasha Kanapé Fontaine ; translated by Howard Scott.
Poems.
Translation of: Manifeste Assi.
Issued in print and electronic formats.
ISBN 978-1-927494-75-2 (paperback).—ISBN 978-1-927494-77-6 (html)
    I. Scott, Howard, 1952-, translator II. Title. III. Title: Manifeste Assi. English.
PS8621.A49M3613 2016   C841'.6   C2016-901839-3
                                          C2016-901840-7

Printed and bound in Canada by Coach House Printing

Mawenzi House Publishers Ltd.
39 Woburn Avenue (B)
Toronto, Ontario M5M 1K5
Canada
www.mawenzihouse.com

Prologue

My forest weeps all alone in silence.
—ALICE JÉRÔME

AND MY *Assi* sitting under my feet drinks this silence.

Assi in Innu means Land.

In the beginning, there is only she. Her womb and her realm. Her cosmogony of both the animal and vegetal kingdoms. The trees, water, wolves and hordes of caribou. Then there is the people. The Innu.

There is me. Strengthened by a new awakening. I will have had to see a movement transform the face of crowds, of my province, of my country before I can achieve this thunderous power filled with spectacular hope.

Precious water. Flowing water. Fierce water.

I dance on the river. Working the rudder of the medicine wheel. My thirst is a manifesto.

Then there is Alberta, Fort McMurray, Athabasca.

Where I stumble. Where I hurt myself. Where I shout the famine of my people.

Where I will say to the whole universe, this world, "Stop the massacre!"

I look around. I don't see my children. They aren't born yet. My grandparents all left without telling me anything. They didn't foresee what would follow. Struggle. Resistance. They are silent, on the other side. They don't speak.

But the spirits dance. They dance on the land.

I receive their visions. Tell me, who today believes in prophecies?

I come from this lineage. The lineage of hunters and braves. I am the daughter of those who walk in dreams. The granddaughter of shamans and healers. The sister of those who speak to the ancestors. I am the one who follows their tracks at -40 degrees Celsius at night, on the shores of the river.

Then, since I am here embracing the soil of my land, *Assi*, I will liberate her womanly songs.

So that the man may once again play the drum. This book declares my love for him.

Natasha Kanapé Fontaine

To my people.
To Assi.

There is a bruise
in the foundation of the world.

Is the path good
for the *nimushumat*?

There's coffee my brother.

The forests recite the names
of every tree

I carve the stone
the gaps spell out the name
of every grub
the stumps

It warps
the land.

Where are you going world
where are you going world my sheets yellowed
by time
where will you run to when the wailing cicadas
when the moon
where will you perish when the reeds

Grumbling
the bears scratch
mud and honey.

I'll write you a manifesto
a love manifesto a paper manifesto

I hear you beating my destiny
the north and south dying
sweating from love among the taigas
the lichens
taint the old customs

Our children are bitter
they have fangs instead of teeth

Hurry up and join me
the tundras are sagging
the mists are rising over the traps

Death is surprising to me
I ponder it
it will have nothing of us.

The reserve
the frightful flakes of storms
*the big fir trees don't die**

I will go carve the history of my clan
on the walls of the bunkers
if we had to
if we are put to death
inch by inch.

*Dominique Demers, *Les grands sapins ne meurent pas* (Montreal: Québec Amérique, 1993).

6

Strike a match
for me
solstice evening

2014 will tremble
the impish winds
the roar of the roads
call to me

I prayed without tobacco
the name of the just

Petakushuat
prophecies of my arteries

Tapue we stand fall down believing
in what can unite the savage dogs
in the beds that we forget
with love.

At the crossing of landscapes
in the stormy race of herds
in the toppling of the world
        through the force of its tramplings
e tipishkat may my body be a mad blast of wind
may I rip apart the last foggy sails
trickling down to your Anticosti deserted archipelago.

What is the dream that I have
my essential birth

The call of the geese
what is the dream
manifesto that I have to write

Where are you going the secret song of the heavens
of the origins of the Pleiades
the squaw maps
hunt your phalanges

My black manes
in the wind of the blond meadows your land

Everything is dream and nothing more will be seen.

What is the dream I have to have
the transparent vision one morning
the dead song of the birds

The buildings crackle
in the break-up of the snows
they don't know how to stoke
        a flame with their fingernails

It is pale the snow of yesteryear
it wore a sea sky face

What is the manifesto
I have to write you.

My dress has an end-of-the-world look
flies over the archipelagos

I cloak
my passion
I faint
cloudy
the dark river
the nations

You had taken me savage
I burned your sheets
Tshakapesh
the fantasies the tricksters
were proclaimed.

I am mixed up the cracked speed my life
I am drunk the secret
the sordid centuries
number beadwork the necks
and the dresses
skip adversity
the pen the birth stand tall
I came into the world three times
the totems the unoccupied pedestal
the unceded peoples.

Don't you hear the obvious
the sulfur
the ember
your skin under
the wreaths of smoke
Athapaskan

The moose tastes so good.

The time is so good the sun
bathes the village blinds the peoples
far farther the hopes and the mountains

I glimpse you crouching
kneeling like a son

Disbelieving of the dawns
disbelieving of the manifestos
barefoot on the meadows and the beaches

The blessed grasses
bend down and straighten up
there is a song the crackling of stems.

A lighthouse is enough to dispossess the boats
the voyages
the river
the storm is brief
I'll write you a thousand unique birds
I'll throw a bottle of rum against your hull
my last breaking

Your legend is a boat full of holes
carried off by the breakers

To silence the incessant song of the seagulls.

The sun lullaby
together we have
dispersed our vultures.

I'll write you
everything I'll shout
every city rooftop
I'll recite
ember memory
nitei mak utassi
my dirty feet singing the beauty
the sand amidst the hourglasses of time

We lose with stagnation
we go mad with dying
at the end of highways 138
beyond reproach

Crazy with dying
at the end of the territory road

My mother weakens
my feet no longer reach her.

You hit your target
you place my heart on your head
bloody crown
inconstancy
drawn from those red books
naume
that we know without knowing

That we read without reading.

The countries surprise
your rough feet

Where archipelagos
run wild wandering wolves
caribou deer
I love you with my yesterday body.

It's time
it's time to come back to the wolves
to the herds
to the wandering shapes

Famine
may you bellow
again
with the return of the untamed

It's time
the springs
the mountains
the smoke

The human.

To give back to my mother *Nikaui*
her origin
tell her I love her
kiss her cheek
a thousand times until the hour of return.

I rocked *Nikaui*
one night I lay down on the fir boughs
along the streets

I stared at the sky

I recalled
the salmon

Harpooned
my departures

My mother sings.

To my mother's mother

I have to shout
so you can soar among the highest swallows
my love is an avalanche.

I am three women in one
I am daughter
mother grandmother

I am my grandmother
my mother
me

I am moon land sea
my memory
my guts my blood
a territorial tremor
a rumbling of ancestors
the heart the emptied wombs

I strike
a huge dried
drum.

I will take my land in hand
I will nurse her
with a piece of cloth
my dress
I will wipe her black tears
and my hair, her gaunt cheeks
will rock her as she shudders
I sleep no more
will put her to sleep on my lap
and wave to my ancestors
stuttering
the yet to be born child that I am.

In the final of the struggles
I will return
sing her
a lullaby
neka

Cree from the West
or the Six Nations

Neka
shash
I have no more battles
to fight.

To the missing women

I hear the bell towers
of your dress of dust
my sister.

Come my spring my maple
reveal yourself
to my flaunted flesh
on your pinnacles

Red winter
glory drums
eager

Fall on your knees
oh hear the voices
we are the messiahs
of our ancestors.

Man of little faith
who never believed in my vertebrae

Knock down my back my limbs
my cross I will bear tattooed to my dirty skins
winter in our great carousing
I am no borderland
     I am numerous multiple nation
multiplied even under your skin of pale redness
at the stroke of the hour my veins
the world is body no you tell me and I neigh
I throw myself without end your spirit you are
my revolution
my madness so delicate dusk *pishimuss*
uashtessiu ma uin—my mother

You couldn't read when I spoke to you of dawn
the parallel
dimension which suits us in our hands
only my life my soul you don't hear
you are
western arrogance in your scenes
my forgiveness
is love and no one
in any crisis I come from
it is impossible they say
to love beyond death

Hope that you may be fierce for us
history I dedicate to you
the last of my songs
the land is sister to the sea

I am the river's adulterous wife
I left my country afar
where my feet are bathed in the ancestors' rest
the foam I use as bleachless soap

Drank the water from my streams
the seaweed buckles
gleam with wonders
there's a celebration tonight
and the creatures under my skirts
so I can dance
so I can stamp my foot among the women
my pain
so I can crush it
and I will make myself woman
        with the eels of my people

I have stifling memory
of the most beautiful forest ruins
        of white moose
my traveler eyes told me
that grandfather is not afraid
he's not afraid
of anything.

The beat of native musics
the tune from Olympus bar I climb
ashtam nimitau whisper
I still have a glass to finish brother
warrior.

I am liberty leading the people
the red lights on the asphalt
your blockaded roads I am your free
wandering resolute in its fate
the solstice
look look me in my earth eyes
my hair loose on your ruined mattress.

All roads
lead to Rome
you told me

All roads
led me to the sun
I told you

And you named me
new world.

I am naked my bed
leaning over the multitude

Promised land
rather like the most beautiful
of desert islands

Forever and ever.

My body
is a

Lair.

I withdraw
the words are bark
where anger has sweated where anger has fearlessly logged
I peeled the intoxication and the froth and foam
with a single hand
winter
did not test you like it should have
did not show you its most potent root
it is said that the world ran all the way here
sticks mark with one line the frozen ground
under the drifting blindfolded
peoples grind the road to be covered:
my grandmother climbed the mountains
the berry is a river in a single fruit
I wash my clothes in a metal ring
I will once again call myself ember and bark
take back my father's name
recall the birth
    of the heavens my people
I will take back the eels
give them back to the sea
I will once again become the land which my ancestors
    built long ago on the banks of the river.

Sometimes [my] heart burns for someone *
absence pulls the strings
my solitude
to the point where I fling myself the storm
drunk the heretical bites of ravenous wolves

My grandmother
bursting with laughter.

* Jean Bédard, *Le chant de la terre innue* (Montreal: VLB, 2014).

One by one they chose me
the boys the tamaracks the Apaches
I will forever mix up my fingers
        the letters their given names
in turn nomad warrior queen
her heart without damp feet on the earth

Then there is he who comes
        the shadow where I see the light
the continent cuts through me

And if I ransacked the gates of the northern plans
undermined the ruins
undid the ancestor land
there would be no more countries
there will be me and my mother
and my sister and my brother and my father
and the others and the others

And the shadow of the countries galvanized in grease
the drums will whisper
        millions of famine shores
I will stamp my foot and I will stamp my ground
with my people the others the songs of peace

We will again frolic the land.

I was asleep on your bed
even if you'd covered me with
hares I wouldn't have been more free
in the middle of opaline nights
we were ebony and garnet our crossing
my frenzy you a strange little room
voodoo books on the shelves
my sight desired your hair and your flags
my person was all burning throated bird
my person swollen by the moon
that women
call red
that has not gone past its fullness

There are my muscles a smooth
leather of your palms
in torment you have
clutched my neck
without my mane your balms

Then there is you lying on the ground
wrapped your fabrics
where you wish me
and at the same time reach me.

I will write you a manifesto
in which I can deliver my empires
my hopes

There is a fire everywhere
in the middle of my chest inside *nitei*.

The ebony and cream castles
built at the bottom of cups
Labrador tea
my table sated with books
you people my dreams my clans

I wake up every day
at the same time

I stand there
the melting of glaciers.

Where are you my negro song
where are you when the city rumbles
when the bridges when the birds
lose their voices from too much north
north where the languages are melting together!
are you my negro when you push
the belly a life
where are you your voice rises when the tree
is cedar while I call you
my song

Do you hear the name of the island I come from
and where you are born?

My disparity
will call to mind your greatness.

My boat
the dawn

Awakened fires
and ritual cries

Our ceremony
was only a blessed night

Freshwater
is walled up
with the arms
of warm mists.

I will write a manifesto
to your dark skin

To your creole rhythm under your tongue
to the song of the drums
on church squares
I will waltz to the rhythm your hands
that strike the woods taut leathers
ten thousand years ago we were the same
we took the water road
the boat is big for love
I don't tell you
and the waves foretell the cruises
where you rule my body

Who said shipwrecks
belong only to sailors?

I am freshwater fish
I am big and beautiful like an eel.

Pleasure is resistance
resistance is pleasure
in your hand
red blood
red framework.

Mitimetau in the footsteps of our ancestors
we walk we walk
        in age of storms
I cross cloven hooves the squalid shore
forever and ever
visions an atoll where I can lie down
        latent worn out and set down
my beautiful, bitter pain
I will deliver my body to silt
where you will manage to love me
        lying along my territories
I sing my most beautiful lullabies
to awaken survival the peoples my mother.

Where are you my song
I baptize myself *mohegankwe*
Anishinaabe it refers to the predator
I will reach the ground that your feet honour
on the feast day
I will wear my finery
　　　—I will make myself beautiful when you come—
so that you may wear your eyes your soul
in my long lands my hands my legs

I will make myself beautiful
with black spruce furs

A poet for her black sun
a fawn look at the Arctics
a hunter of his territory wife
a woman of the *atik^u* clan
with a modern arrow bullet
in her marrow.

The moss
gets wet in the rain of wonders
the world is beautiful
you dwell in the glow
your pupils *ussit* my visions *nitassi*
manifestly.

My head rests on your arm
I am an Ungava fragment
without ochre
nor torrent

My trees are the 9th of January
on the sides of streets
anite nutshimit
crude oil
in my lungs
an endless riverbank
my universe

I am black mineral exceptional
the Manic dam and its cavernous hands
my coinciding history
a few beavers

My grandfather
returned *nuash* waters
eternal lands

My head rests on your arm
following rites
older than the world
celebrating the astral essences

My soul surge to the exhausted woods.

Our ancestors walk
climb up and down
they came with the master

She is beautiful my mother
if you saw her

All those rivers below span
the giants of those legends
my boots
dried in the sun

Looks like you're alone in the air
to love.

Confetti maples
it's a grandiose tale
your bone structure
your free falls
give drink to my deep gorges
along your smooth skin
your mouth the honey

Gentle your words my lips
the room is big for love
open window
grassy lane in winter
the sheets exist bogs
subarctic mixed the branches
our hands allied
finally scratches born

The space is big for love
the window the light green lane in winter
so gentle your words my lips

And the song of the drums.

My madness the world
the bit between my teeth
my love his dark skin
wreaths of smoke
incisive industries
the country the colours combine
dirty water of paintings
my pale skin
fools my people
their quest for the sun

I will be a country for me alone
I have children with an invisible father the sky
the thunder
I will reach
the depths of vertigo

The inhabitants make
unwarded children
they raise virgins lunacy
I dream the days of suns
my people dance
around combustions.

I will present a huge fire
I will burn the residential schools
the paper acts

And with a single gust of wind
brush away every pipeline
the caribou will come
running with the buffalo
the horses the deer
there will be a great trembling

The caribou
the buffalo the horses
the deer will come
with the land
drown the pipelines

We will burn
the residential schools
the paper acts

We will embody
a huge fire.

Over there battles call to me
you are everything that is born
everything that explodes
millions of percussions reverence
on the day of death and trembling waters

Curl up connected to the corner behind my teeth
so painful to say nothing
to whisper nothing
to the creature one's body loves
so rough my love my time
where battles call to me
it's not time to whisper my madness to him
it's not time either to settle down

My word subsists with sage my beloved
the times are coming
when the book will appear.

Let us soak in silence
wet are the cities
where we burn
where we wait
where we sleep
where we dance
on tangled sheets
drunken eyes.

The solstices
appear

Look east
isn't it calling us?

Tomorrow I will go at night to fish for eels
the wake of foliage the milky buildings
marble and cobblestone the age-old pitfall
has built us flippers and scales
to deprive the master of heaven

Be my shadow so I don't break
I tremble like the earth when the sky gets drunk.

Nitakushin
colossal my loss

Anticosti my rosary
balls of foam
my fierce beauty Mingan
my howling beast

You love
your abdomen is wet
under my sheets ivory coasts

The lullaby
of the sun.

When I write you this manifesto
there I'll be

When I see a hole the clouds
I am flush with the lands
in bird ore
there in the hollow of the
battles that dry up lips
there where tears are just and they sweat
rivers without dams
there where we conjure up the
mortar giants of the republics

My love you don't know
my soul is a fire on the bay

You are my struggle my revolution the peoples
that I can see the clouds my passion
you're the poem
interlaced with my fingers my deer.

I will wait for you
a promised land

I will sing
the dark mouth

The burned-out estuary.

Who sprinkled the fields of heaven?
an immutable hope
gets moving bitumens and horned feet

I have a land to die
with magnetic prairies
the tall wheat raging
the toxic blond waters

Where my skirts are hanging
where my manes are falling in love
where my anger hangs.

A sacrilege
captivate the vertebrae from heaven with my outbursts
your shoulder blades on my stage dancing all around
our fire vibrating our flesh
boiling with fever

The night is red
nitshishkueikun
the giant road calculated

Do you receive me
I curled up your huge antlers

The polar ice caps chase
their tails the bone I gnaw while
delaying the springtimes of the world
Montreal the white wolves run
under the acrid tsunamis of the cities
before they are reached
I will tear off their fur survive them

You don't hear
my bones crack
when I stand up.

Exile
lives here

He crosses the walls
from time to time, he comes

I don't force him to enter
he doesn't force me to enter

Sometimes I wait for him
sometimes I take him out
sometimes I hear him
sometimes I marry him.

Uashat
the table is set
the salmon smoked
the sunshine abundance

Culture consoles
the bruising of the river

The oil drinks the water
Montreal
could make out the song of the geese
will they dare come back?

Atik^u sees me
among the foliage the ropes
smoke a prayer

Say I want you
don't hide anything
it's good

I say to him only a caribou silence
I'm only waiting for your call

You no longer people the dreams of anyone
you pounce with a cry of love my guts
my countries my drenched culture
we cross the suffocating memories
you camouflage your frost
would you have farther than the masts the torches
embraced the north in my place

Are you trying to reach the south in the coming hour?

The 138 is blocked
the keys somewhere.

Song to *Papakissik*[u]

I vibrate caribou
your ice roads your sandy lands
your ropes your throw songs
your land harnesses your lichen
the cold with its imposing fronts

I vibrate caribou
your loves tundras your legend beards
your ravenous wolves with ocher blood eyes
your life sweeps me away your wind freezes me
the herd will eat me

Crowned head with pallid storm
love me my master fill my belly
so that I can wait for the moon wait for you
for the steaming foam to lay me down.

The herds
drowned recklessly
opened my veins
I gave them my spilled
blood my ancestors
have watered the country

The Master
knew the offering
fed the soil.

I am this black-blooded land
I am a burnt throat
a buried land
another white-armed one
my hands have nails
broken from
pounding the earth
a snake conceals me
I wipe my mother
her gray tears
I am this black-blooded land
I have cancer in the left lung
I have cancer in fourteen torrents
I have cancer in the crazy tribe

Exodus

The drums
cannot soothe
my mother.

I am the woman who falls from the sky
the swallow of the vultures
the deformed hill the melting icecaps
the maniac of jails calamities
fingers on my eyes
I kiss you as if
you were a brother

I am the woman who falls from the sky
the battles are oil black
the flags tear at every footstep
no one's heart still beats in the street
no one still fights on the road
no one still with their face painted red

I am the woman who falls from the sky
I have sown nothing to feed my hope
I have kept nothing for myself

Matter space body
legs swing feet on asphalt
the universe is large for love
where are the moorings I throw off
the bristling tundra
I have no more island to lie down on.

Blend of black land my land Assi

I return to the black heart of my land I want to drink
to the sleep of its name
—PAUL CHAMBERLAND

I black burst in the grass
the grass of ancient songs in tons on the wheat
the fields
Wounded Knee my heart Athapaskan
my Romaine soul
Oka

Nitassinan

Nin
Innu land
land *Assi*
Innu-*Assi*

Land Quebec
I make the journey the wrong way from my exile
nitassi my moorings my sublime
the beach salt eats away at the rust of your winged mouth

land! land promised to my father by the Father
where are you hiding the vibrant packs
    of the east and west?
where are you hiding the smoking sails
    of the north and south?

I'm in pain

my belly aches
my belly of the land aches

They write me words
which I could not speak

It is difficult
to *manuscribe* the present
in stone

Where is the sound of your voice when the universe blazes
before my eyes
when the universe trembles
when the universities
      seem to forget the footsteps on the land?

THE LAND, DAMMIT!

I wept, wept for the goddess
they build pipelines everywhere they forget
we'll be called "petrol wood"
"bleach cunt" "you want my
pipeline in your mouth"? the others would say

If I'm not the one
yes I'll eat up Enbridge
      and all the other filthy carbonics
because I'm famined
because I'm famined with living

5 now 6 million in the city
and no one calls me

between your body and the tip of your arm
let's go around in a round dance together
hold my hand tight
        in the black grass at night
I'll sing until the sulfur dawn
        of the gloomy day
my brave land

I have black shattered
I have black smoked in the summer grass
heart in hands hands in earth
I heard yours beat until
the armoured surface of the hard-working herds
your horrid machinery
on our glassy skins
your damned illusions
and your crimes bury enough to shut my people up
I have black fury loved in the grass
under the cloven hooves of the bison herds
my heart in your hands your hands in my land

My soiled dress my black feet
my veins devoured by innocent moons
they are blinded my sisters my mothers
they no longer hear the wolves aging
write letters redden my feathers
towards the heart of the archipelago island of nations

Here the sky is so blue
my heart so black so crude so explosion within
too full of your steep railroads
your vicious snakes on my island my Turtle

I have black burst in the grass
the grass of ancient songs in tons on the wheat
the meadows
Wounded Knee my heart Athapaskan
my Romaine soul
Oka

I have red written my red fear
wailed my choked back rage.

Idle no more
under a snowy sun

Our steps of clay and glory
the monstrance lethargy
is at its end
its famine

Shash tau
pishim^u.

Among the dying trunks of the land
I will offer my heart to *Assi*

She will be my mother
my wealth
my reason to live
my dirty drug
my undrinkable liquor
my restorative tea

My brothers' grandmothers
will blind me with their grievances

My grandmothers will say to me again and again
Assi Assi Assi (land)
and I will answer
eshe eshe eshe (yes)
I will hang up the phone
I will have nothing more to say
my forest weeps all alone in silence
and the rivers and the lakes
and the creatures
and the spirits.

Assi
lives

The poem is here
a manifesto
it will mark time

A circle is defined
an aura the moon
a halo the sun

I will return people of water
I will spit out fourteen torrents
I will swallow three moons
to better drink the milk of my mother.

Glossary of Innu words and phrases

p. 2: *nimushumat* – grandfathers

p. 7: *petakushuat* – they are heard
tapue – really, it's true

p. 8: *e tipishkat* – it is night

p. 11: *Tshakapesh* – central character in Innu legends

p. 17: *nitei mak utassi* – my heart with its land

p. 18: *naume* – that in the distance

p. 21: *Nikaui* – my mother

p. 26: *neka* – mama
shash – already, finally, that's enough, it's done, that's all

p. 29: *pishimuss* – month of December
uashtessiu ma uin – autumn light

p. 31: *ashtam nimitau* – come, let's dance

p. 40: *nitei* – my heart

p. 47: *Mitimetau* – the path of our ancestors

p. 48: *mohegankwe* – (Anishinaabe) wolf woman
atik^u – caribou

p. 49: *ussit* – on the surface
nitassi – my land

p. 50: *anite nutshimit* – there, in the bush
nuash – as far as, up to, until

p. 58: *nitakushin* – I feel sick

p. 62: *nitshishkueikun* – it's driving me crazy

p. 64: *Uashat* – Innu reserve adjacent to the city of Sept-Îles, literally "on the bay"

p. 66: *Papakissik^u* – name of the guardian spirit of the caribou

p. 70: *nitassinan* – our land
nin – I, me, myself

p. 74: *Shash tau / pishim^u* – it is already there / the sun

Born in 1991 in Baie-Comeau, NATASHA KANAPÉ FONTAINE is Pessamit Innu. Slam poet, painter, actor, and indigenous rights activist, her first book, *N'entre pas dans mon âme avec tes chaussures* (*Do Not Enter My Soul in Your Shoes*) was published in 2012 in French, and in English by Mawenzi House in 2015. In 2013, the original French version won the poetry prize of the Society of Francophone Writers of America. *Manifeste Assi* was first published in French in 2014 by Mémoire d'encrier. Natasha Kanapé Fontaine lives in Montreal.